Mandie Davis

illustrated by
Alain Blancbec

Published by Les Puces Ltd
ISBN 978-1-9164839-2-7
© March 2019 Les Puces Ltd
www.lespuces.co.uk
Original artwork © January 2018 Alain Blancbec & Les Puces Ltd

Also available from Les Puces

Visit the shop on our website at www.lespuces.co.uk

 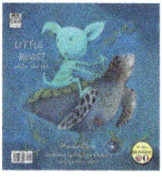 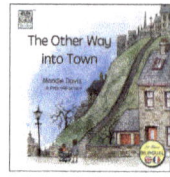 

 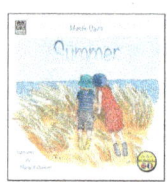  

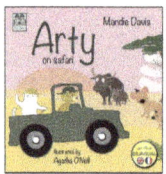 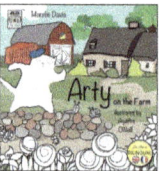 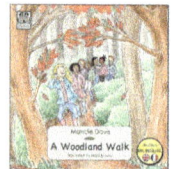  

The Cheeky Crow lives on the tallest pine in the green forest. Today the sun is shining and the sky is blue. The weather is nice. The Cheeky Crow loves days like this. It's the perfect day to be good.

Normally the Cheeky Crow loves flying around the beach and making a mess, but today he is trying to be good!

He flies out to sea. The sea is blue and deep, and the sky is blue and endless. The Cheeky Crow is daydreaming and now he's flown too far. He is tired. Ah! the perfect spot. "I'll just rest here for a moment" he thinks.

Oh no! What's happening?! Suddenly the Cheeky Crow is moving very fast. He's water skiing! He holds on tight until he is near the beach…

...then he flies off out of control.

Round and round he spins and lands...

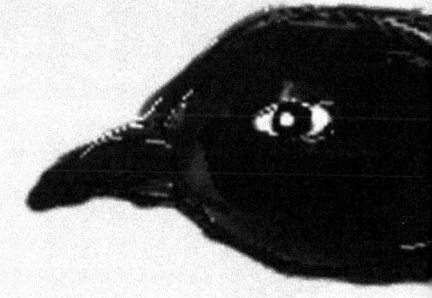

... in an ice cream! Oops! Sorry!

Can the Cheeky Crow ever be good?!

Normally the Cheeky Crow loves flying round the countryside and making a mess, but today he is trying to be good!

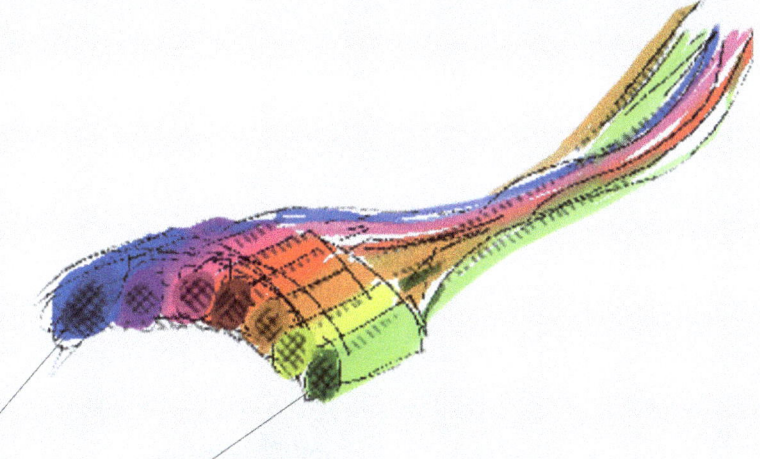

Today is a windy day. The trees are waving and leaves are flying around. The clouds are racing across the sky. The Cheeky Crow decides to race with them. He flies faster and faster until...

Oh no! He's tangled in a kite. Round and round, down and down, he spins and lands in a haystack. Luckily the Cheeky Crow is safe but the kite is broken. Can the Cheeky Crow ever be good?!

Normally the Cheeky Crow loves flying round the town and making a mess but today he is trying to be good! It's a stormy day, with thunder and lightning. It's raining but the Cheeky Crow doesn't mind. He loves the rain. He likes to see all the brightly coloured umbrellas.

He sees a beautiful red umbrella lying next to a park bench. "Perfect" he thinks as he flies down to investigate.

Oh no! At the same time as a crash of lightning, the umbrella snaps shut around The Cheeky Crow. He struggles but manages to escape although he is soaking wet and a little nervous of umbrellas now!

Flying back home to the tallest pine in the green forest, the air turns colder and the Cheeky Crow realises it's been snowing. It's cold. He looks down and sees a wonderful snowman that some children have made in a field. At the last minute, the Cheeky Crow decides to have a closer look, but he turns too late! He flies like an arrow straight for the snowman...

Crash! He lands right in it! Poor Cheeky Crow! He will have to wait for the snow to melt before he can escape.

After all his adventures the Cheeky Crow wants to get back to his nest in the green forest. The snow and rain have stopped and the sun is trying to come out again. There is a beautiful rainbow high in the sky as he finally arrives home. He settles down to rest. He has had a day full of adventures.

The next morning the Cheeky Crow wakes to find the forest covered in fog. Today isn't a good day for flying around or for having any more adventures. The Cheeky Crow decides to stay in his nest. Do you think he can be good today?

في صباح اليوم التالي استيقظ الغراب المشاكس ليجد الغابة مغطاة بالضباب. اليوم ليس يومًا جيدًا للتجول أو لأية مغامرات أخرى. قرر الغراب البقاء في عشه. هل تعتقدون أنه من الممكن أن يحسن الغراب سلوكه اليوم؟

بعد مغامراته، أراد الغراب المشاكس العودة إلى عشه في الغابة الخضراء. توقفت الأمطار والثلوج وحاولت الشمس الخروج مرة أخرى. وظهر قوس قزح جميل عال في السماء، ووصل أخيرا إلى منزله. واستقر للراحة. كان يومه مليئا بالمغامرات.

وتم الاصطدام، مسكين هو الغراب المشاكس. فهو الآن عالق ولن يتمكن من الفرار حتى ذوبان الثلج.

في طريق عودته إلى منزله في أعلى شجرة الصنوبر في الغابة الخضراء، أصبح الجو بارداً، ولاحظ الغراب المشاكس بأن الثلج يتساقط. نظر الغراب إلى الأسفل ووجد رجل ثلج رائع صنعه الأطفال في الحقل. في آخر لحظة، قرر الغراب المشاكس التحقق بنفسه، لكن بعد فوات الأوان! وطار بشكل مستقيم كالسهم نحو رجل الثلج..

آه لا! عندها وفي نفس الوقت مع حدوث البرق، سكرت المظلة حول الغراب المشاكس لكنه تمكن من الفرار على الرغم من انه مبلل بالمياه و مزاجه سيئ.

عندها لاحظ مظلة حمراء جميلة بجانب إحدى المقاعد في الحديقة. "رائع" فكر لنفسه وقرر ان يطير ويتحقق بنفسه.

من عادته يستمتع الغراب المشاكس بالتحليق فوق المدينة وإحداث الفوضى. لكنه اليوم يحاول أن يغير سلوكه وأن يكون جيداا! إنه يوم عاصف وممطر، رعد وبرق. لكن الغراب المشاكس لا يمانع. فهو يحب المطر. كما يحب أن يرى المظلات ذات الألوان الزاهية.

آه لا! تشابك الغراب مع طائرة ورقية وبدأ يدور ويدور، نزولاً إلى الأسفل حتى وقع في كومة قش. لحسن حظه لم يصبه مكروه، لكن الطائرة الورقية انكسرت. لا يمكن للغراب المشاكس أن يحسن سلوكه ويكون جيداً.

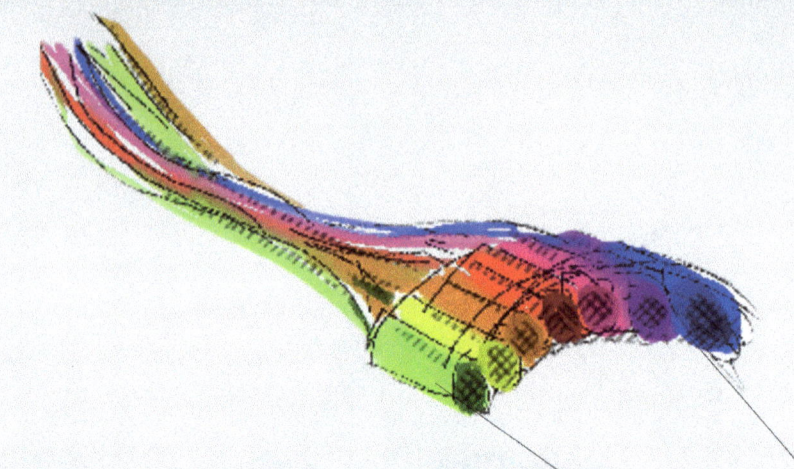

اليوم يوم عاصف. الأشجار تتمايل والأوراق تتساقط. الغيوم تتسابق عبر السماء. قرر الغراب المشاكس التسابق معها. فطار وأسرع وأسرع أكثر حتى ...

من عادته يستمتع الغراب المشاكس بالتحليق فوق الريف وإحداث الفوضى، لكنه اليوم يحاول أن يغير سلوكه وأن يكون جيداً!

في قرن البوظة!! آه ثم آه! للأسف! لم يتمكن الغراب المشاكس من تغيير سلوكه!

...ثم فقد السيطرة. دارَ ودارَ وغطَّ..

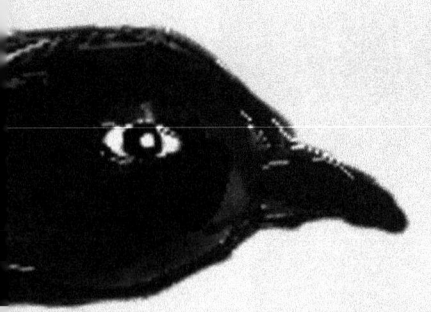

آه لا! ماذا حدث؟! فجأة طار الغراب المشاكس بسرعة! حاول التمسك والتزلج على سطح الماء حتى وصل بالقرب من الشاطئ.

طار الغراب فوق البحر. البحر أزرق وعميق، والسماء زرقاء. والغراب المشاكس استغرق في أحلام اليقظة ووصل إلى مدى بعيد. وشعر بالتعب. "هذا المكان مناسب سأرتاح قليلاً هنا"، قال لنفسه.

من عادته يستمتع الغراب المشاكس بالتحليق فوق الشاطئ وإحداث الفوضى. لكنه اليوم يحاول أن يغير سلوكه وأن يكون جيداً.

يعيش الغراب المشاكس في أطول شجرة صنوبر في الغابة الخضراء. اليوم الشمس مشرقة، السماء زرقاء والجو جميل، إنه اليوم الأفضل لتغيير سلوكه والتصرف على نحو جيد.

الغُرَابُ المشاكس
يحاول تغيير سلوكه!

من Les Puces أيضاً

www.lespuces.co.uk زوروا موقعنا على الإنترنت

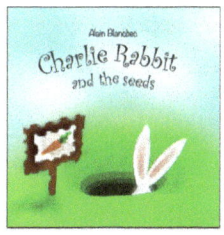

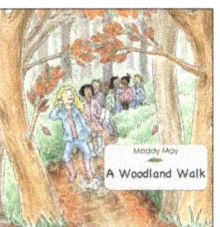

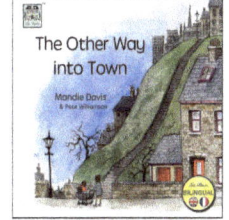

ماندي دايفس

الرسام القصصي
ألان بلانبيك

Published by Les Puces Ltd
ISBN 978-1-9164839-2-7
© March 2019 Les Puces Ltd
www.lespuces.co.uk
Original artwork © January 2018 Alain Blancbec & Les Puces Ltd

www.ingramcontent.com/pod-product-compliance
Lightning Source LLC
Chambersburg PA
CBHW042028100526
44587CB00029B/4335